Lost Lake

Folk Opera

November 2013   **Volume 1 Number 1**

In This Issue

Folk Opera talks to **John Davis,** architect of the citywide arts campus grand plan, and we take a careful look through Folk Opera Glasses at the road that brought him here.

Commonweal resident artist, **Scott Dixon,** offers a critical look at Edgar Allen Poe's final days in a scene from his full length play.

Looking for Lost Lake 9

An investigative history unravels the dam mystery, by Folk Opera editor **Tom Driscoll**

Lost Lake Folk Opera

Lost Lake Folk Opera is a Shipwreckt Books imprint
published three times annually.

115(B) Parkway Avenue   Lanesboro, Mn 55949
507 458 8190   contact@shipwrecktbooks.com
Managing Editor   Tom Driscoll
Publisher   Beth Stanford

www.shipwrecktbooks.com

Cover photo of Lanesboro falls by David Tacke
Cover montage of John Davis & Lanesboro falls by Tom Driscoll

My Father's Trees

By Mary Lewis

Today I pick the last of this year's spinach. Gone to flower the leaves get bitter and yellow while the young beans I planted around them on my last visit surge into verdant adolescence. My father's garden is at its midsummer peak when it drinks its longest drafts of the sun and the tomatoes that sulked through May take hold of the earth and grow from it at the same time. The riot of green soothes my city nerves, still raw from the traffic on 35W. On my first job out of the U, this place still feels more like home than the one-bedroom apartment I shared until last week, with Martha. What is left of the day flames in the hazel bushes Dad and I planted years ago, but the sun withdraws without devouring them.

Mary Lewis has written for R.K.V.R.Y. Quarterly, Persimmon Tree & Wapsipinicon Almanac. She lives in Decorah, IA.

I turn to catch the first nighthawk peent in his tumbling flight before he vanishes behind the windbreak elms on the north side of the farmhouse. That's where my little brother Davie and I made campfires and put up tents of blankets and broomsticks that always fell down before the night turned to morning. He'd put a flashlight in his mouth to look spooky, and I'd tell him stories about an escaped con with a gold arm ten times stronger than his real one that could grab you right out of the tent.

We boys were close as un-thinned carrots then. I don't know where he is now, and Dad doesn't either. We choose not to fear the worst, but something mild, like he can't find a job and feels so ashamed he can't talk to us.

Inside I open the icy metal spigot of the big glass jar that brewed tea in the sun all day, but now sits in the fridge next to the unhusked peas. I plop a couple of ice cubes in my glass but suck on one the way Mom told me never to do because it was impolite.

Once, years back, I pressed my tongue against the handle of the old water pump in January because Davie dared me, and I stuck there till Dad poured water over my startled mouth to release me. I can still see him from the corner of my eye because I could not turn my head, running towards me down the icy path from the farmhouse. Mom made me stand over the old porcelain sink with a warm washcloth to sooth my face. My damaged tongue tasted its own blood on the rough nap of the terrycloth.

Today I hold to my hot forehead a cold washcloth as I stand over the stainless steel sink, a trick for the heat I learned from Mom.

"See you still know how to cool off, it's been a hot one." Dad strides into the kitchen and gives me a slap on the back.

I can always tell when he is near, just by the smell of sweat and gasoline that clings to his coveralls. Maybe that's why I never mind filling up.

"Thought you might be here, but I had to finish tilling." He drinks a glass of water it in one long slug, his eyes fishlike on either side of the upturned glass.

"I left work early, so I had time to do a little weeding in the garden. How does the corn look?"

"Held back by too much rain, but starting to come out of it, except in the low places. Should have a decent crop if we don't get washed out again." Crop talk comes easily for both of us, and we carry on that way while he splashes water on his face and scrubs his hands. I have a job with a software company, but it is hard to explain the work I do.

"You're looking good Evan, your Mom always said you'd be taller than me, and so pretty you'd have to swat the girls away like flies." He slugs me in the shoulder like I knew he would so as not to be too mushy, but I don't return the gesture.

"What's the matter boy, I always get slugs back." I give him one, but he looks me over and sits me down. Then he pulls a pot out of the fridge and puts it on the range. "Spaghetti, it's always better the next day."

We sit at the big round table that still has little dents from when Davie and I pounded the table with the pointy ends of our fork handles like Vikings demanding mead. That didn't last long because Mom took away the forks and gave us plastic spoons for our spaghetti.

"You know a fork is the best tool for spaghetti," I say.

"Just slips off a plastic spoon, doesn't it?" Dad smiles but then his chewing slows and his eyes go soft.

"You still miss Mom, don't you?" I didn't mean to say it, but something in the curve of his mouth gives me courage. Dad puts down his fork and leans back on the hind legs of his chair, stretching his legs out in front.

"Guess she'll just always be a part of me." It is a voice I'd never heard before, low and hoarse, the kind of voice you'd use with an intimate friend, not a son.

The table, range, cabinets I knew so well seem drained and pale, like they belong in someone else's kitchen. I place my hands on the table to have something to hold on to.

I do not tell him Martha had left for a job in Chicago, great pay, intensive care unit at Passavant. But nurses could work anywhere, what's wrong with Mayo, or Fairfield or Gunderson? Fine places all, but not the specific experience she wanted, she had said, sipping ice tea, a curtain of long auburn hair hiding her face. I can feel the smoothness of her hair in remembered strokes.

"I miss her too." I let the weight fall on me and it is almost better than holding it up all this time. When it happened I was the one who watched the tractor turn over and raced to find her pinned under it up to her waist. I was fourteen and gaining muscle but you can't move a 5300 Deere unless you're Superman. The strain of trying to push it off her still lives in my body. She shook her head and beckoned me with her unpinned arm. She called me Evie like when I was little, and stroked my hair, and said how glad she was that I was there, but not to remember her like this. When her hand dropped my tears drained my body.

Dad sold the tractor and never mowed that slope again. He wasn't even interested in harvesting the corn, so the neighbors did it for him, but no one picked the apples that year and the deer got fat on fallen Connell Reds and Haralsons. We ate a lot of frozen pizza and Davie and I learned a couple of dishes from Aunt Jenny, like mac and cheese, meatloaf, and spaghetti, but Dad wasn't good for much for six months. Then one spring Saturday when the snow still dappled the fields he found me sprawled on the couch and said, "Let's go prune the Russets."

Dad lets his chair come down for a landing and fiddles with the spaghetti, but doesn't put much more into his mouth. "You know if it wasn't for you boys I don't think I could have kept on living." His voice still has that raw sound, but like it is struggling to be normal.

Toads start their chirring chorus down by the pond, and I want to race through the goldenrod till the smell of black pond muck becomes part of me. I need to pour into my skull the deafening sound of toads in love, and I don't want to listen to my father's hurt, because he never saw my own.

"Dad, I know you're in pain, and maybe always will be, but have you any idea what Davie and I went through? I was there when she died for God's sake. I couldn't free her. Can you even imagine my guilt?"

"There's enough of that to go around Evan, I could have kept her from mowing there in the first place."

"Why is it so important to you that you hurt the most? To prove your love? To cover up certain indiscretions?"

Dad knocks his chair over as he stands up. I stumble out of mine and he backs me to the wall with one hand raised. He'd never hit me in his life.

"I can't believe my own son is repeating such foul rumors."

"If they're rumors why did you hide from them?" I know I am a couple of inches taller than him, but it never sinks in until that moment when, our faces inches apart, I look down into his eyes. I didn't believe it before Mom died, but later I understood he'd had an affair with Wanda, an old girlfriend from high school. I'd seen them laughing together at Fletch's Café, and one winter he'd be able to pick us up after school a lot because he'd be in town so often.

Dad looks up at his raised hand and lets it fall. He collapses into a chair, puts his head in his hands and releases hoarse sobs from the bottom of his lungs. I sit down again and wait. After some minutes he says, "We were angry at each other for a time, and I went to Wanda for solace. But I never stopped loving your Mom."

"Some way to show your love," I enjoy hurting him.

"I never told her about it."

"But of course she knew because everyone did. Even your sons put it together eventually."

"Evan, I have to live with the torture that I never got to say what I truly felt. Judge me all you want, but grant me that understanding."

I say some stupid adolescent thing like "whatever" and stomp off to bed. I lie awake most of the night while the moonlight from my window streams over me.

I get out of bed when the gray daylight strengthens over the silver moonlight, and wander out to the orchard. As a kid I'd race from the school bus to hide amongst the apple trees where no one could find me for chores. I'd lie on my back to gaze up past the long grass around me into the mountains of clouds. One day an apple fell from the old Macintosh and rolled near my ear. I did not turn my head to look because a wasp buzzed over it and they get mean in the fall. It was so close I could hear it burrow into the wormholes to lap up the sweet thick juice.

Now I tromp through the long grass that soaks my jeans with dew, and see Dad waving to me from up in the trees, like he thinks everything is just fine. I think about turning around, but I walk towards him, slowly to show I am still angry, and when I get to the Golden Russet I climb up next to him. Both of us red-faced, me from my outrage and the climb, him from the work and what I hope is guilt.

Not a good time of year to prune, but you couldn't always get a chore done in the season that fit it best. He has a saw for me and we work in our own corners of that big apple tree without saying a word. When we swing to the ground dripping sweat we lie on the grass looking into the trees 'til our breath comes slowly and together without our trying. Maybe that's why the hardness in me begins to soften. Could be it is because Martha left and now I know more about that kind of sorrow. Or else I am just tired of the anger and don't want to punish my father any more.

"Dad, there's something I never told you about the worst day of our lives. I kept it from you because at first I didn't understand it, and when I did, to punish you. I don't know if I'm sorry for not telling you, but I think now's the time."

I can hear Dad hold his breath.

"After she said she loved me, she pulled my head close to hers with the arm that wasn't pinned down. And you know what her last words were, Dad?" We both keep looking up at the apple leaves or I couldn't have finished. "She said 'make sure to tell your father that I forgive him.' Then she took a deep breath and a little blood came out of the corner of her mouth and she said 'with all my heart.'" We lie without moving for a long time, but I can hear my father crying.

On the day I leave, once more I walk through the apples and there near the Russet in the matted grass something casts sunlight to my eye. My saw. I had left it, like a memory, to fend for itself.

Against my thigh I wipe the bits of rust that formed overnight on the blade, careful not to tear my jeans with the teeth. Solid to my hand I grasp the handle and swing it in long arcs to match my stride that takes me through the dappled shade of my father's trees.

Looking for Lost Lake
By Tom Driscoll

Woman on the hill overlooking Lost Lake circa 1870

Spring backwards a few hundred years. It's March. The muddy Root River sashays unconstrained. No fields cultivated to the river's edge, no highways, bridge abutments, parking lots, riprap dikes, just wetlands to absorb high water. Wood Ducks flap their wings wildly overhead, skimming the treetops. Red-eyed males splashed with purple, green, bronze, and white feathers, and crested females, camouflaged brown-gray, swoop down to dabble for insects in a calm pool. Already paired to breed, the Wood Ducks make their annual journey north along the meandering river in search of hollow-bellied trees within waddling distance of fresh water for duckling waders that will hatch on a bed of downy breast feathers in late summer.

Tom Driscoll, Managing Editor of Folk Opera & Shipwreckt Books, lives in Rushford, MN.

High bluffs look down on the north end of a future Lanesboro as the waterfowl turn south and zoom upstream. The left bank will one day become Parkway Avenue. At the foot of Church Hill, where Sons of Norway will build a meeting hall, the river flows east through marshy flats now occupied by Sylvan Park, then loops sharply around the site of today's elementary school.

Colorful as a Renaissance still life, Wood Ducks flock west to the bluff where narrow Ox Trail Road now shinnies around a quarried rock face high above the river. Veering south, the migrants disappear into a natural bowl sheltered by hillsides cropped with old hardwoods and eroded limestone. Back then, river crawled from the west a good 25-feet below the water level behind the dam today.

Imagine immigrant Wood Duck hunters in the forested bog west of Lanesboro, farmers, loggers, railroad builders eager to make the most of the opportunities America offered. Someone with a good eye noticed that plugging the narrow crack in the bowl near town would flood the south fork river valley with even more opportunities.

"Water power to turn millstones?" I asked Lanesboro's resident historian, Don Ward. "Fillmore County farmers grew a lot of wheat?"

"True," he explained, "the first of three flour mills was built in 1870. But by 1890, depleted soil and wheat rust forced farmers to switch to new crops and livestock. Lanesboro Townsite Company built the dam in 1868 because they wanted a big lake, over 500-hundred-acres it was, two-miles-long, half-a-mile-wide, 35 feet at its deepest.

While the valley filled up, Townsite built the Phoenix Hotel for $50,000. Very luxurious for 1870. In 1874, they diverted the river to run behind Main Street, eliminating two bridges on the road into town."

"Lanesboro expecting a flood of tourists?"

"Townsite investors hoped rich Easterners would come here to build summer homes on the lake. The Phoenix provided a fancy place to stay during construction."

"Any of those summer homes still standing?"

"None were ever built. The lake was popular though. Fishing, canoeing, ice-skating. But it started getting shallow. Eventually, erosion from logging and agriculture completely silted it in. By 1900 the lake was gone. Silt's 30-feet-deep in places. For the last 50 years, Lost Lake's been a Game Refuge."

I first heard about the Lost Lake Refuge from DNR Area Wildlife Manager, Gary Nelson, and Fillmore County Conservation Officer, Dan Book, when they informed me of plans to decommission, or vacate, the State Refuge.

The name snagged my interest. "There's a lake out there?"

"Don't know. Our records show that in 1954 county residents petitioned the DNR to set aside roughly 900 acres for a State Game Refuge. About all there is in the file."

"So why vacate the refuge now?"

"It's private land. Hunters confuse it with State Forest."

"But no one should be hunting on a refuge anyway, right?"

"That depends. State Parks and State Lands are game refuges. These days of course we manage wildlife populations.

Deer and small game are thriving, so in-season you can hunt at Lost Lake."

"You said it's privately-owned."

"And that's the problem. Some hunters see that State Game Refuge sign and think they can ignore No Trespassing signs. DNR wants to vacate the refuge, accommodate these landowners, clear up a confusing situation. The refuge serves no useful purpose."

One of those landowners, Duane Benson, explained the problem. "You see a No Trespassing sign, you know what it means. But then down the road you see a State Game Refuge sign. What's that mean? What's a Game Refuge? It's terribly confusing."

Confusing is right. The very idea of taking game in a State Refuge confuses some.

Looking for Lost Lake at the Lanesboro museum, I met Irene Strom. Irene told me a story about her husband who had been an avid hunter. Years earlier, he'd tracked a wounded deer into Lost Lake. "In those days you couldn't hunt in the refuge," Irene confided. "Game Warden caught my husband with the deer out there and wrote a citation!"

Curious to see the rules, I went to the Minnesota Legislature website. According to Statute 97A.085, a Game Refuge may be designated "only if the commissioner finds that protected wild animals are depleted and are in danger of extermination, or that it will best serve the public interest." At least for the past half-dozen years, lawmakers have authorized seasonal hunting at Lost Lake.

Lost Lake: not a lake. Game Refuge: not a refuge. No hunting: hunting allowed. Now I really was confused.

Then I spoke to Wilbur Hall. In 1955, Wilbur started farming 114 acres on the west end of Lost Lake. "I think it was the Gun Club's idea to set up the refuge. No hunting squirrel, deer, pheasant. Wasn't sure I liked it, but if I recall correctly, they wanted to protect Wood Ducks."

WOOD DUCK by Dana Gardner. From *Living in a Dream: Bluff Country Offerings*, a **Lost Lake Folk Art** book by Nancy Overcott.

Wood Ducks! Suddenly I had found Lost Lake, time slowly eroding the unbridled Root River of yesteryear, fallow wheat fields, fizzled economic plans, institutional memories faded, waterfowl on the brink of extinction, the past buried under 30-feet of silt at Lost Lake.

Menander Drowns in the Bath
By Jon Welsh

Once–once–once there was a strict line to follow;
seeding furrows on contoured hills, flat and fallow plains,
regiments behind their colors, parties lashed by whips,
chained rowers below deck stroking, stroke, stroke.

Men–mostly–men took the lead, took and held advantage
cloaked in flowing robes. Priests, barristers, sheikhs.
Sometimes knights girdled in armor, ungainly as robots.
Holding the bone of the pen, a sword, a spear
stiff in their hand they thrust authority about
following the stiff line, the stiff line they learned.

No more. The battle joined, a more supple complement
surges forward, flows around, under, over -
not dressed in mythic garb or undressed
but making myth a mirthful exercise.

Men become boys, pushed to the side.
History unseated rewrites the rules;
clouds once advanced along a front
break up, dissipate, recede
like a hairline above a wrinkled brow.

Who gleams, whose eye sparkles now,
who is she, no mystery no more
yet not yet master or mistress?
Once – once stories told and foretold
came to a certain end, an end
now uncertain but in the retelling
of old tales, wives' tales,
fishmongers' wanton wives,
had some conclusion.

Bone separates from flesh –
where once the line was straight
it is more sinuous in the sea, fluid,
knows how to get around
as do women who have made an end of men.

**Jon Welsh is the author of two books
of poetry, *Reversal* and *Beatitudes &
Holy Rollers*, both from Undine Press.
He lives in Arlington, VA.**

A MIDNIGHT DREARY

Scene from an original play **By Scott Dixon**

CAST OF CHARACTERS:

Edgar Allan Poe, 40. Author, editor & critic in his last hours

John Allan, Poe's foster father

George Graham, publishers

Dr. Moran, Poe's deathbed physician

Longfellow

Virginia Clemm, 20. Poe's wife & cousin

Frances Allan, Poe's foster mother

Elizabeth, Poe's mother

Nurse, Poe's deathbed attendant

Rufus Griswold, a fellow critic & editor

Uncle Galt

Scott Dixon is a resident artist with the Commonweal Theatre Company in Lanesboro, MN.

In this scene, POE's consciousness is experiencing two memories simultaneously, attending to his wife, VIRGINIA, at her sickbed while encountering GRISWOLD at a dinner party.

VIRGINIA: You should be getting ready.

POE: I have some time.

VIRGINIA: Will lots of people be there?

POE: I certainly hope so. Where are your slippers?

VIRGINIA: In there.

(POE goes to the wardrobe to retrieve them. On the opposite side of the stage, PARTY GUESTS begin to arrive, talking and laughing.)

VIRGINIA: *(Continues.)* Do you see them?

POE: Oh, yes. Here you are.

VIRGINIA: Would you put them on for me? *(POE nods and puts the socks on her feet while stealing glances towards the party.)* What is it?

POE: What?

VIRGINIA: What are you looking at?

POE: Nothing.

VIRGINIA: *(Coughing.)* If you need to go.

POE: No, no. Not yet.

GRISWOLD: *(Emerging from the crowd at the party.)* Edgar.

POE: Rufus.

VIRGINIA: Eddy.

POE: Yes, dear?

VIRGINIA: Tell me again when you're leaving for Philadelphia.

POE: I don't know if I'm going at all now.

GRISWOLD: Allow me to extend my sympathies for your wife.

POE: Thank you.

GRISWOLD: How is she?

POE: Well. She's resting.

GRISWOLD: So, the entire room is abuzz. A new magazine from Edgar Allan Poe. Have you a title yet? I'd be happy to suggest –

POE: The Stylus.

GRISWOLD: Very nice.

VIRGINIA: They always liked you in Philadelphia.

POE: Sorry?

VIRGINIA: Why aren't you going?

POE: I couldn't leave you alone.

VIRGINIA: *(Coughing.)* You don't want to lose the theatre deposits.

POE: I don't care.

GRISWOLD: Excuse me?

POE: Does George Graham know you're here?

GRISWOLD: I don't know if he does or not. I came to hear you read.

POE: No, they came to hear me read.

VIRGINIA: Eddy –

POE: I'm here.

GRISWOLD: Then you tell me why I'm here.

POE: What business does the fox usually have in the hen house?

GRISWOLD: I see. I'm here to feast on your investors.

POE: You've taken food from my plate already when you took my job with Graham. And for more money, too. Well done.

GRISWOLD: You resigned. Over one article. George needed someone immediately and I was available. And since I was present when you resigned, he didn't have to embarrass himself explaining what you had done to a stranger. You disappoint me.

POE: I disappoint you? And who are you that I should be mindful of that? Who are you? What have you done?

VIRGINIA: Eddy, please, you're shouting.

POE: Sissy, why didn't you tell me?

VIRGINIA: I didn't have to.

POE: I didn't know.

VIRGINIA: Yes. You did.

POE: *(Beat.)*   Yes, I did.

GRISWOLD: You may not believe this, but I'll be happy for you if you succeed.

POE: If I succeed?

GRISWOLD: Edgar, think about who you're talking to. I know what you have and have not been able to raise for your magazine down to the penny.

(VIRGINIA has a violent coughing fit.)

POE: You need some water. I'll get you a glass.

VIRGINIA: Thank you.

(POE crosses into the world of the party where he gets himself a tumbler of water.)

POE: And have your amazing powers of precognition given you insight into what will happen tonight?

GRISWOLD: Not precognition. The wisdom of experience. If you make twenty dollars, I'll be surprised – nay, astonished.

POE: And why is that?

GRISWOLD: You've never understood who you're dealing with. This is a room full of businessmen and they only give their money to a man who knows how to spend it.

POE: Are you saying I don't know how to run a magazine?

GRISWOLD: I'm saying you'll never get that far. These people won't give a damn about your prospectus when you're standing before them in a frock coat that doesn't quite fit and a shirt that's going threadbare at the cuffs.

POE: Will you let me by, please?

GRISWOLD: I'm trying to help you.

POE: Help me? By God, you imagine you can insult me and then be thanked for it?

GRISWOLD: I beg your pardon!

POE: Step out of my way.

GRISWOLD: Very well then, don't believe me. But consider for yourself what these businessmen will think about what you did with "The Raven". Listen to me! It gives me shivers every time I read it, and you printed it in a newspaper! You gave it away! At best, it makes you look like an eccentric.

POE: And at worst?

GRISWOLD: You confirm your own worst gossip. I mean, look at yourself, man!

POE: What do you mean?

GRISWOLD: That glass hasn't been out of your hands all night.

POE: It's water.

GRISWOLD: Oh, Edgar. For shame.

POE: You don't believe me? *(Throws the contents of the tumbler in GRISWOLD's face.)* Go to hell.

GRISWOLD: You petulant child. If time and place were convenient, I should take you over my knee. *(Exits.)*

VIRGINIA: Eddy?

POE: *(To the party guests.)* Forgive me.

VIRGINIA: Are you still there?

POE: Ladies and gentlemen, I beg your pardon –

VIRGINIA: I feel so heavy. Like I'm falling into myself.

POE: - and I ask that you excuse the outburst of a temperamental artist.

VIRGINIA: I just need to hear your voice.

POE: If you would indulge me and my passions for a little longer, I would like to present you with a piece of one my works, THE RAVEN.

Once upon a midnight dreary, while I
    pondered, weak and weary,
Over many a quaint and curious
    volume of forgotten lore,
While I nodded, nearly napping,
    suddenly there came a tapping,
As of some one gently rapping, rapping

at my chamber door.
"'Tis some visitor," I muttered,
"tapping at my chamber door-
Only this, and nothing more."

Ah, distinctly I remember it was in the
    bleak December,
And each separate dying ember
    wrought its ghost upon the floor.
Eagerly I wished the morrow; - vainly I
    had sought to borrow
From my books surcease of sorrow-
    sorrow for the lost Lenore-
For the rare and radiant maiden whom
    the angels name Lenore-
Nameless here for evermore.

O, Mr. Poe

And the silken sad uncertain rustling of
    each purple curtain
Thrilled me- filled me with fantastic
    terrors never felt before;
So that now, to still the beating of my
    heart, I stood repeating,
"'Tis some visitor entreating entrance at
    my chamber door-
Some late visitor entreating entrance at

my chamber door;-
This it is, and nothing more."

Presently my soul grew stronger;
hesitating then no longer,
"Sir," said I, "or Madam, truly your
forgiveness I implore;
But the fact is I was napping, and so
gently you came rapping,
And so faintly you came tapping,
tapping at my chamber door,
That I scarce was sure I heard you"-
here I opened wide the door;-
Darkness there, and nothing more.

Deep into that darkness peering, long I
stood there wondering, fearing,
Doubting, dreaming dreams no mortals
ever dared to dream before;
But the silence was unbroken, and the
stillness gave no token,
And the only word there spoken was
the whispered word, "Lenore!"
This I whispered, and an echo
murmured back the word, "Lenore!"-
Merely this, and nothing more.

Back into the chamber turning, all my
soul within me burning,
Soon again I heard a tapping somewhat
louder than before.
"Surely," said I, "surely that is
something at my window lattice:
Let me see, then, what thereat is, and
this mystery explore-
Let my heart be still a moment and this
mystery explore;-
'Tis the wind and nothing more."

Open here I flung the shutter, when,
with many a flirt and flutter,
In there stepped a stately raven of the
saintly days of yore;
Not the least obeisance made he; not a
minute stopped or stayed he;
But, with mien of lord or lady, perched
above my chamber door-

Perched upon a bust of Pallas just
above my chamber door-
Perched, and sat, and nothing more.

Then this ebony bird beguiling my sad
fancy into smiling,
By the grave and stern decorum of the
countenance it wore.
"Though thy crest be shorn and
shaven, thou," I said, "art sure no
craven,
Ghastly grim and ancient raven
wandering from the Nightly shore-
Tell me what thy lordly name is on the
Night's Plutonian shore!"
Quoth the Raven, "Nevermore."

Much I marvelled this ungainly fowl to
hear discourse so plainly,
Though its answer little meaning- little
relevancy bore;
For we cannot help agreeing that no
living human being
Ever yet was blest with seeing bird
above his chamber door-
Bird or beast upon the sculptured bust
above his chamber door,
With such name as "Nevermore."

But the raven, sitting lonely on the
placid bust, spoke only
That one word, as if his soul in that one
word he did outpour.
Nothing further then he uttered- not a
feather then he fluttered-
Till I scarcely more than muttered,
"other friends have flown before-
On the morrow he will leave me, as my
hopes have flown before."
Then the bird said, "Nevermore."

Startled at the stillness broken by reply
so aptly spoken,
"Doubtless," said I, "what it utters is its
only stock and store,
Caught from some unhappy master
whom unmerciful Disaster

Followed fast and followed faster till
his songs one burden bore-
Till the dirges of his Hope that
melancholy burden bore
Of 'Never- nevermore'."

But the Raven still beguiling all my
fancy into smiling,
Straight I wheeled a cushioned seat in
front of bird, and bust and door;
Then upon the velvet sinking, I betook
myself to linking
Fancy unto fancy, thinking what this
ominous bird of yore-
What this grim, ungainly, ghastly, gaunt
and ominous bird of yore
Meant in croaking "Nevermore."

This I sat engaged in guessing, but no
syllable expressing
To the fowl whose fiery eyes now
burned into my bosom's core;
This and more I sat divining, with my
head at ease reclining
On the cushion's velvet lining that the
lamplight gloated o'er,
But whose velvet violet lining with the
lamplight gloating o'er,
She shall press, ah, nevermore!

Then methought the air grew denser,
perfumed from an unseen censer
Swung by Seraphim whose footfalls
tinkled on the tufted floor.
"Wretch," I cried, "thy God hath lent
thee- by these angels he hath sent thee
Respite- respite and nepenthe, from thy
memories of Lenore!
Quaff, oh quaff this kind nepenthe and
forget this lost Lenore!"
Quoth the Raven, "Nevermore."

"Prophet!" said I, "thing of evil! -
prophet still, if bird or devil!-
Whether Tempter sent, or whether
tempest tossed thee here ashore,

Desolate yet all undaunted, on this
desert land enchanted-
On this home by horror haunted- tell
me truly, I implore-
Is there- is there balm in Gilead? - tell
me- tell me, I implore!"
Quoth the Raven, "Nevermore."

"Prophet!" said I, "thing of evil-
prophet still, if bird or devil!
By that Heaven that bends above us- by
that God we both adore-
Tell this soul with sorrow laden if,
within the distant Aidenn,
It shall clasp a sainted maiden whom
the angels name Lenore-
Clasp a rare and radiant maiden whom
the angels name Lenore."
Quoth the Raven, "Nevermore."

"Be that word our sign in parting, bird
or fiend," I shrieked, upstarting-
"Get thee back into the tempest and
the Night's Plutonian shore!
Leave no black plume as a token of that
lie thy soul hath spoken!
Leave my loneliness unbroken! - quit
the bust above my door!
Take thy beak from out my heart, and
take thy form from off my door!"
Quoth the Raven, "Nevermore."

And the Raven, never flitting, still is
sitting, still is sitting
On the pallid bust of Pallas just above
my chamber door;
And his eyes have all the seeming of a
demon's that is dreaming,
And the lamplight o'er him streaming
throws his shadow on the floor;
And my soul from out that shadow that
lies floating on the floor
Shall be lifted- nevermore!

(End of scene.)

THE RAVEN, by Edgar Allen Poe, was first published in 1845.

A MIDNIGHT DREARY was developed and produced in 2009 with support from The Commonweal Theatre Company.

What might have happened, if it had
By Haley Thompson

All morning sitting here, facing
the walnut tree, the arbor you made

winding one tree into another.
The arbor, it bends over the summer squash.

Remember how the seeds felt. Your hands
pulling weeds. All morning sitting facing out

sketching your feet on the porch-rail and the brush
fields behind them. The house beyond that

has no one to paint it. The chimney still smokes,
occasionally. The house you sit outside of

there's no one to answer the way the wind hits it.
The tear in the screen has curled and opened, into

the shape of a flower someone once brought you.
A black-eyed Susan? Peace lily for your wedding.

Off toward the walnut tree the bark is open,
where you thought he was living, once in a dream.

Haley Thompson, author of *Home is a Place worth Burying*, published by the UP ON BIG ROCK POETRY SERIES, earned an MFA in Poetry from the Iowa Writer's Workshop. She lives & teaches now in Nashville, TN.

Stalking Rhubarb

From the novel by **Solveig Blegen**

"I'm the one who's got to die when it's time for me to die, so let me live my life the way I want to." - Jimi Hendrix

Rhubarb Johnson scrutinized Edna's spidery handwriting on the yellowed index card that he had kept tucked in his backpack for the last forty years.

He loved rhubarb so much that he had even named himself for it years earlier. He felt it suited him, the sourness, which he kept hidden, the stringiness of his ectomorph physical build, that he kept buff with weight lifting, and the sweetness and crunch of additions to this life of his Lord and the Lord's work, deadly as it sometimes was.

Solveig Blegen, English teacher, entrepreneur and freelance writer, lives and serves on the library board in Spring Grove, MN.

Rhu measured, crumbled, sliced and diced, stirred, and layered. The dessert was soon ready for the oven. In the hour that it baked he attempted to make order of the kitchen, and then sat on the little patio-walkway in front of the apartment sipping his instant coffee. Looking up, he noted that several ladies schlepped toward the second floor laundry in their bedroom slippers and housecoats, pink sponge curlers adorning their hair. Indeed, the pot luck tonight was a big deal and these women wanted to look their best.

Rhubarb's thoughts then veered toward his problem at hand, the

---

RHUBARB'S DESSERT

Crumb Topping:
1 cup sifted flour
¾ cup rolled oats (oatmeal)
1 cup brown sugar, packed
1 teaspoon cinnamon
½ cup melted butter
Mix ingredients until crumbly. Press half of the crumbs into a greased 8" x 8" or 9" x 9" pan. Cover with:
4 cups rhubarb, cut in ½ inches

In a saucepan combine:
1 cup sugar
2 tablespoons cornstarch
1 cup water
1 teaspoon vanilla
Cook, stirring until thick and clear. Pour over rhubarb. Top with remaining crumbs.
Bake in moderate oven (350 degrees) for one hour. Cut into squares, serve warm, plain or with whipped cream or perhaps ice cream.

---

necessity of sending Louise, Edna's daughter, to her Eternal Reward. How? Her demise had to be very carefully executed. He wasn't in a position to flee to another ARR community, especially with his car, Big Bertha II, ailing. His roaming eyes suddenly fell on a blooming oleander shrub growing in the center of the courtyard. Oleander? Oleander? What did he know about oleander? He knew that it was poisonous and not even the wood should be used for cooking as it gives off poisonous fumes. Aha! This was his answer. He would make a pretty salad of the oleander leaves mixed in with the arugula, a tasty dressing, and further enhance its appearance with the petals of the pink flowers.

Perhaps it would be wiser to find oleander shrubs other than those in the courtyard, mused Rhu. Harvesting leaves and blossoms there could be a tip off to the occupants of the many apartments facing the courtyard. He casually meandered to the front of the building and spotted several more shrubs in far less conspicuous areas. Whistling softly, he deftly plucked a handful of leaves, a few blossoms from a corner shrub, and placed them in the ever-handy zippered plastic bag stuffed in his trouser pocket. He straightened, looked around, and seeing no one, he breathed a sigh of relief. Wait, what was that dark shadow in the walkway in the far corner of the building? Upon closer inspection, he realized it was an elderly man he had seen earlier when he was having his coffee. Tall and very thin, the old man wore striped bib overalls, which was strange attire for Florida. But the man appeared vacant and vaguely delusional so Rhu decided he posed no threat whatsoever.

"Louise, Louise, Sweetheart," called out Rhu as he entered apartment 122, "Could I borrow your car again for a run to the grocery store?"

Louise's wild-haired head poked out of the bedroom, "Sure thing. The key is sitting on top of my red handbag by the door. Whatcha need?"

"Oh," replied Rhu, "I have such a yen for another good salad. Besides, I don't want to eat a heavy meal before the pot luck. Does a light salad sound good to you?"

"Sure does," responded Louise. She adored fancy salads but rarely had the financial resources to indulge.

Louise's faded red Camaro was a bitch to start, but Rhu remained patient and the engine soon roared to life. Skirting the deepest potholes, Rhu headed down the road thinking about the poison salad. He would delay the light lunch so the first symptoms of toxicity would start about the time of the pot luck. That way, there would be enough other components in her stomach to make it harder to identify the deadly ingredient. Also, she would be surrounded by other seniors he had charmed, so he wouldn't be considered the instigator of her death. Good plan. Praise be to God. "I put my trust in you and you give me the tools to do your work," he mused.

He whistled *Delia's Gone*. Soon he was singing, "Delia's gone, one more round, Delia's gone," and drumming his fingers on the steering wheel. Who needed a CD player in the car? Not Rhubarb Johnson! He was multi-talented and ever so grateful for his chance for one more round.

SUSAN

"To be successful we must build inner strength. The key is to keep nourishment going into your mind on a daily basis. It can be just a little bit every day, but to overcome the negativity that exists in our society we need to do that."
- Greg Smith in *Speaking of Success*.

Susan had a burning desire to first strangle Mary and then to take her job and shove it. She was far too exhausted to be driving to Sarasota with the miniscule amount of sleep she had had. In addition, the towering mountain of work sitting in her office that haunted her was supported by frantic calls from the ARR main office demanding this document or that. She kept giving emphatic replies to the affirmative for each request with a date, that even in her wildest dreams, she knew she'd never be able to satisfy. If she weren't so busy and so fatigued, she might feel guilty.

She had cancelled her visit to Crystal Bay the previous afternoon as she had neglected the conference call regarding a new *Inherit the Earth* project. And, yikes, she had been asked to do a Power Point presentation regarding its progress, which she barely finished before the appointed time.

Unfortunately, most of it was hype. She would soon have to visit the site in Orlando to verify the facts she had spouted so confidently.

Why did she tend to think in obscenities when she was tired, and do things, say things she would never do or utter when she was well rested? Why had she said what she said to the heavy man getting out of the dirty green Mazda in the parking lot as she was going into Target to get a Verona dark roasted coffee from Starbucks?

His Wisconsin license plate read 299 UCK. As she was prone to do with license plates, she formed a word. Sometimes it was an acronym. Today, unfortunately, it was a word. Before her caffeine starved brain kicked in she had asked the chubby man, "What happened to the 'F'?"

"It's being used by assholes like you," barked the ruddy Wisconsin man.

"Oh, I am so sorry," said Susan with mock apology. "I see now that it was an L not an F," and she quickly moved on. Susan, chastened by her embarrassing initial comment, went through the steps of her self-devised Happiness Makeover.

First, she had to choose happiness. She had learned to believe that happiness was gained through achievement, not given her as a gift.

Second, Susan needed to think of and enumerate five things for which she was grateful. This truly did pull her away from being bitter.

Third: She must come up with someone she needed to forgive. That was easy, she forgave Mary for calling her a Viking bitch just yesterday.

Fourth, she had to squelch all her negativity, both thoughts and feelings. She forced herself to find a core of serenity and then breathe in and out until she felt calmness permeate her being.

Fifth, she needed to remind herself that shopping for more things would not promote happiness. She had everything she needed and she knew that the acquisition of even more meant giving up the clean, sleek lines she loved in her home in addition to having more stuff to clean and maintain.

Sixth, Susan realized that she needed to hone more friendships to give her life the palpable richness it lacked. And new friendships could not be with her managers. Managers could never be true friends as they were likely to curry her friendship for job security.

Seventh and last, she must endeavor to engage in more meaningful activities. Well, she was doing just that. What could be more meaningful than helping provide decent housing for the ill, poor, and needy elderly?

Feeling better, Susan reviewed her next activity, the trip to Crystal Bay.

Yesterday when she had cancelled her property visit with Mary, she had heard a distinct sigh of relief in Mary's voice. Then, as she held onto her phone a second longer, which occasionally brought her unexpected but valuable information, she heard Mary say to someone, "The Viking bitch isn't going to make it."

"Viking Bitch, huh?" It wasn't the label she minded so much, it was Mary calling her a Viking bitch. She thought they had a pretty decent relationship, and, she had just forgiven Mary, so she told herself to just drop it.

This morning, however, a frantic tone laced Mary's voice as she begged Susan to pay a visit to Crystal Bay. Could she come immediately? Yes, it was vitally important. Please.

Stuart was comfortably parked in Mary's office when Susan walked in. Stuart? The fellow that Mary and she had taken to Straight Way Village? Does it seem a little cozy here?

Mary stood. "Hi, Susan," she smiled. "I may be out of line asking you here, but Stuart discovered something that both of us find disturbing." Mary appeared to have calmed down since her 6 a.m. phone call.

"I know I shouldn't have done this, however, I did allow Stuart to spend the night in Rhu's vacated apartment last night. He's waiting for his check. He's out of funds. And I have not heard a word from Rhu since he left and said he didn't intend to return. At any rate, Stuart found something in Rhu's apartment that we think is scary."

"What's that?" asked Susan, feeling even wearier and as yet not particularly concerned.

"A newspaper clipping from Milktown, Wisconsin – about the death of Stuart's mother."

"That seems pretty coincidental," Susan reacted. "I don't understand why it's so frightening."

"You don't think there could be a connection between Rhubarb Johnson and the deaths in Daytona, Leesburg and here?" Mary asked.

"Myself," interjected Stuart, "I'm wondering if his real name isn't Clarence, Clarence Johnson. My mother once hired a young man by that name to help on her farm not long before she was smothered. He wasn't charged with her death, but he must have moved on quickly because all the animals were left without food and water. Mother spoke highly of him. She said he was *such a nice young man*, high praise coming from her. I've spent my life looking for him, because the killer was never found. It was him killed my ma," exclaimed Stuart. "I'm certain."

"I just checked again and Rhu's given name on his housing application is Clarence. I didn't pay much attention initially because by the time people get to be 62 years old, most of them have nicknames," added Mary.

"Hmm," Susan responded, "when Rhu asked about an apartment in Leesburg, we suggested he check with Nancy at Straight View. I can't help but wonder why he is sticking to ARR communities if he is guilty of murder. Does he feel more assured of references and less paper work with ARR?"

"We've got to call Nancy right away," exclaimed Mary. "I know he's renting from her. She called me yesterday, asked me to fax the reference form for him, which I did. Oh my God!" Mary's head dropped into her hands.

"No!" Stuart cried. "Louise is there too. And she would take to a sweet talking newcomer like a duck to water."

They quickly called Nancy who confirmed that Rhubarb Johnson was still at the apartment complex. She said his old car had major problems. Plus, his background and credit checks had not yet cleared. Susan worried that Nancy had succumbed to Rhu's charm, which was not good. Nancy mentioned how much she looked forward to seeing Rhu that very night at the monthly pot luck. "He's going to bring his *famous* rhubarb dessert!" gushed Nancy.

RHUBARB

"When eating a fruit, think of the person who planted the tree." - Vietnamese Proverb

"Dear Lord, I need a blessing. Right about now. Sometimes it's hell trying to do the Lord's work," whispered Rhubarb Johnson.

It was hot. He was sweating. Hot, hot. Okay, Rhu, he told himself, calm down, forget about the Florida heat, concentrate on the job at hand, and praise the Lord. He needed to pick up some salad ingredients with rather strong flavors to mask the oleander leaves. Delicious fruit. Something refreshing. Berries. Grapes. Mango. And lime juice. And fresh mint. Yes. That would do it. Praise the Lord.

"So if your woman's devilish, you can let her run, or you can bring her down and do her, like Delia got done. Delia's gone, one more round, Delia's gone." Rhu sang as he set the plastic bag on the passenger seat of Louise's Camaro.

Flash! A thought crossed his mind. Maybe the Camaro could replace Big Bertha-II. Nice V-8 engine. Bitch to start, but he could tinker with that. Down the road he would have it repainted. The rust and faded red finish didn't quite fit with his self-image. Or maybe he would trade it in on a hog. Now, there was a thought. He pictured himself roaring down the highway wearing leather pants, a caramel brown shade of Nice 'n Easy embedded in his gray pompadour. Oh, now that was cool.

"Mr. Johnson. Mr. Johnson!"

Was that Nancy's voice he heard? Yes, indeed it was. Rhu rounded the corner of Straight Way Village, passing close to the lobby and office. But he was sweaty and eager to assemble his salad.

"Mr. Johnson, your credit and criminal checks have cleared and I also ran your lease and 50059. Would this be a good time for you to sign them?" asked Nancy.

"Good morning, Miz Nancy," greeted Rhu. "Would you mind terribly if I came back later to do all that? I kinda have my hands full at the moment." He lifted his hefty bags and smiled ruefully. "Would shortly before the pot luck be convenient for you, Miz Nancy?"

Oh, I am brilliant, thought Rhu. I can feed Louise her salad, stop in the office to sign the lease while Louise slowly becomes sick. Louise can bring my rhubarb dessert to the community room and I can be an innocent bystander when I arrive late from signing paperwork.

"That will work," Nancy replied. "I won't be able to send your certification to TRACS right away, but that shouldn't make any difference. I'm hoping to finish up here so I can go to the pot luck. Did you know that managers need to be invited to be able to attend pot luck?"

"No," responded Rhu. "Why?"

"Darned if I know," Nancy chirped. "I just heard it from Mary. When she wants to attend a pot luck, she has to ask a resident to invite her. Must have something to do with the fact that it's a resident activity, not a management affair."

"Well, now that I am soon to be a resident, I solemnly swear to always invite you to pot luck," promised Rhu. "By the way, what is TRACS?"

"Oh, it's the property management software HUD uses to track the certification of folks living in HUD subsidized communities. Web-based. It's a pain in the butt if somebody's income doesn't perfectly match their records. It's all tied in together with Social Security and banks, I suppose," explained Nancy.

***

Rhu watched as Louise tied the sash on the once-lovely red knit wrap dress and adjusted the sweetheart neckline. Her silver sandals had numerous black scrub marks, but somehow they lent elegance to Louise's diminutive frame.

"How do I look?" Louise twirled wearing an impish smile.

"Outstanding," replied Rhu with sincerity that surprised him. Realizing that this would be her final wardrobe attempt made his eyes mist. She could have been a lovely creature, he sighed to himself. But, but, he reminded himself, he was doing the Lord's work for her benefit, and she was Edna's daughter and that tie must not remain. Think about the red tie on her wrap dress and how it could symbolically strangle him.

Louise relished Rhubarb's oleander salad, savoring each slice of mango drizzled with fresh lime juice. She commented on how the mint leaves set off the flavors of the fruit. Ironically, the leaf on her fork at that moment was an oleander leaf. Rhu himself enjoyed delectable salad – minus oleander leaves, of course.

"Holy Shit!" exclaimed Louise. "This is good."

Rhu thought she might actually lick the bowl clean.

Suddenly, Louise turned up the volume on her old red radio. She started shimmying to *Toxic* by Britney Spears, red knit fabric swirling around her hips. She repeated the words, "*You're toxic. I'm slipping under … with a taste of poison paradise …*" Hot song, thought Rhu, a cold shiver shooting up his spine.

LOUISE

"I don't like food that's too carefully arranged; it makes me think that the chef is spending too much time arranging and not enough time cooking. If I wanted a picture I'd buy a painting." - Andy Rooney

"Steady, steady there," Louise muttered to herself, balancing the dessert pan on her arm – rhubarb crisp – while adjusting the shoulder strap of her stringy black bag. She held the screen door open with her butt as she closed the door and snaked her hand around the door to turn the lock.

Ah, to heck with locking up, she thought to herself. Rhu will probably come back with his lease papers anyway. And if someone comes by to steal something, I'll have an excuse to make a stink about it and get some attention, maybe sympathy.

In the corner of her eye, Louise saw something move down at the end of the building then realized that a creepy old man she had seen before skulked in the shadows. Was she being stalked? Why would he be peeking at her? She shook her head, adjusted her grip on the heavy dessert, and continued toward the community room on the second floor. Although she felt certain the elderly man was demented, his eyes didn't look as vacant as she would have expected. Jeez. It almost seemed like his eyes sought hers, trying to communicate.

"Yoo-hoo, Louise!" Louise looked up to see Lydia and Agnes waving at her from the second floor walkway.

Lydia asked, "Got that rhubarb dessert?"

"I sure do," replied Louise as she reached the elevator door, punched number 2 and waited. And waited. "What is wrong here?"

Suddenly, the ancient elevator lurched and began its brief ascent. Louise felt her stomach tighten. God, she hated elevators. The door creaked open and she stumbled briefly on the threshold. Great, she had a new scuff on her third hand silver sandals. Why couldn't elevators stop even with the floor? Her stomach didn't like the little jolts.

What was going on with her stomach? She had eaten so well the last twenty-four hours. And she hadn't consumed anything alcoholic. She grimaced briefly recalling a lapse of honesty in Minneapolis one time when she saw what she thought was a case of wine in the backseat of silver Corvette. Believing it was piggy for the owner of that lovely car to have a whole case of wine, especially when she had none, Louise opened the car door, grabbed a bottle and stuffed it quickly into her madras hobo bag.

A couple hours later, she peeled the gold foil off the neck of the bottle, unscrewed the top, and poured the pale liquid into one of her cloudy plastic tumblers. In her eagerness to consume the liquid gold, she hadn't paid much attention to the viscous consistency of the wine before gulping. Turns out it wasn't wine at all. It was olive oil. She looked at the label on the slender dark bottle and read, "Produced in eastern Tuscany in the Chianti Classico area in the classic Tuscan style of olive oils."

"Ah, shit." Shit had become the word to describe that evening. And the next morning too, hung over after drinking a whole bottle of wine. Then she was hungry. But there was no food in her tiny apartment. Hell, she didn't eat food anyway, not when she could drink her calories.

"Over here," screeched Agnes from across the room. "The desserts go on this table."

"Okey dokey," responded Louise. She felt strange. Not only did her stomach continue to lurch, but she felt disoriented. Seemed like she wasn't really there. And Agnes and Lydia's voices started fading away as she got closer to them. Was she going to faint? The last time she fainted, it was from sheer hunger. That certainly wasn't the case now. She'd just eaten Rhu's delicious salad. Oops! Something nasty was going on. She felt and smelled a certain telltale spread of diarrhea in her lace panties.

Louise dropped the rhubarb dessert on the table none too gently and turned toward a public restroom luckily only a few feet away. Inside, she immediately faced a difficult decision, whether to sit down quickly on the stool or to lose her cookies in the sink. Okay. Sink first.

As she heaved bouts of her lunch salad, and that morning's cereal, Louise suddenly felt so weak that she clutched the sink in an effort to stay upright. The room started spinning and she realized she wouldn't make it to the stool. How embarrassing. Damn. Why had she eaten so much in the last twenty-four hours? The room spun faster and faster. Her knuckles turned white as she gripped the sink tighter. Quickly, Louise crumbled to the restroom floor. Her throat burned. Could she have strep throat again?

Somehow, that didn't seem likely, nor did it explain the vomiting and diarrhea. She would just close her eyes for a little while until the urgency of the next vomiting purge arrived. She would just lie still while the room twirled around her. Let the merry-go-round spin without her. She would just lie still.

"Louise, Louise," Lydia hollered, "Are you okay in there?" Louise heard voices outside the door. Had she locked the bathroom door? She didn't want anyone walking in on her personal mess. Oh, lordy, lordy. Was she going to die? Is this what dying felt like? She made a supreme effort to raise her head. She had to lock the door. Oh, no, this time she wasn't going to make it to the sink. She heard the voices again, not only Lydia's but also somebody else. Who was it? Well, shit. Literally, shit. As her bodily fluids seeped out, Louise sank back to the floor, not caring one iota about her ruined red dress and lace panties. She would just lie here until darkness took over.

SUSAN

"The purpose of setting a really big goal is not so that you can achieve it so much, but it's who you become in the process of achieving it." - Jack Canfield

Susan's eyes fell on Mary's nervous pleating and pleating again the bottom of her leopard print skirt. For once Mary wasn't chattering. Neither was Stuart. As Susan increased the pressure on the accelerator, she changed lanes, passed semis, lawn care vehicles, and Lincoln town cars on I-75. She prayed she wasn't too late. Yes, Mary and Stuart had convinced her that Rhubarb was not the person he had professed to be. His travel and appearance seemed to square with the deaths at each property. His method of killing differed each time. However, none were violent and he used his charm to gain access to each woman. What didn't make sense was his professed religion. Did he believe that his actions were in accordance with his beliefs? Somehow, Susan felt that must be his truth. The yellowed newspaper clipping that Stuart had found was the decisive factor. How ironic. What are the odds that Stuart and Louise's mother would also have been Rhu's victims?

Susan increased her speed and watched the odometer climb to 85-mph. If she were stopped by Florida's finest, she would ask for assistance at Straight View. Oh for heaven's sake. Why was she not requesting assistance right now? Pulling her cell phone from her jacket pocket, she hit 911 and reported a possible murder attempt at Straight View. Using her most authoritative tone she insisted that, of course, she was positive that this could be happening and that she was speeding on I-75 right now, hoping to arrive before anything drastic happened. Please, please meet her there.

Mary looked absolutely ill. Susan knew that Mary had really liked Rhu and found it difficult to believe that he was anything other than what he seemed. Mary didn't tend to get too fond of her residents. However, when one broke through her barrier of indifference, she believed they could do no wrong.

Stuart drummed his fingernails on the center console in the back seat. He seemed poised for flight, ready to bolt for Louise's apartment the second they arrived at Straight View parking lot. Even though he had issues with Louise's past life style and her tarty ways, Louise was Stuart's only family and he would be devastated to lose her. He saw himself as her protector. Stuart never got over his mother's death and the horrible situation he had walked into all those years ago.

Susan decided not to call Nancy as that might alert Rhu. If Rhu ran, he might not be apprehended and could go on to murder again. She understood that Rhu had charmed Nancy as he had charmed Mary, and Nancy would be reluctant to believe ill of him. Nancy tended to find the best in everyone.

This was delightful and part of her charm, but it was also annoyingly naïve. She recalled one of her first conversations with Nancy when Nancy admitted that she hadn't used sun screen when she first moved to Florida. Why? Because when she was outside she was usually in a moving car. Yes, a convertible. The assumption was that the rays of sunshine couldn't keep up with her. Duh!

Her phone rang just as *Blues Mania* came on the radio and broke the tension. "Yes, this is Susan."

"Susan, it's Victoria from HUD. What on earth is happening with your properties?" Victoria shouted.

"Well, what are you referring to?" Susan countered cautiously.

"I'm referring to an unusual number of resident deaths. And they don't seem quite 'natural'. I'm getting calls from residents and they are extremely upset. Are you even aware of this?"

"Oh, I am very aware of this. But I really don't know what to tell you, Victoria. I am involving the police and, of course, there will be investigations. Right now, I am trying to get to Straight View just as fast as I dare drive. I suspect that there is a potential problem there."

"What makes you think that?" Victoria demanded.

"Victoria, it's a long story. I really can't take the time now to fill you in. However, I promise you I will keep you informed as I can. Please try to soothe the residents that are calling you. We will take care of things." Susan hung up and steered around a lawn maintenance truck that was dawdling at 70 miles per hour. Grass must be growing more slowly this time of year. Susan's fleeting thought evaporated quickly.

Sirens shrieked behind her as she turned onto Lemon Road, taking the curves almost on two wheels. Please, God, let all the residents be safe, she prayed silently. Susan had a distinct feeling that Mary and Stuart were praying the same words.

It was 4:50 p.m. The pot luck, she had learned, would start at 5 p.m. sharp.

Emergency vehicles with screaming sirens tore right up to the entrance and drivers shoved their vehicles into park as they jumped out. The race to save a life was on. Susan, Stuart, and Mary all tried to swallow large lumps of panic, slow their racing hearts, yet pacify their minds so they could think clearly and ascertain what they could do.

STUART

"Whether one eats a cat or not is a personal choice, and I don't want to sway anyone one way or another. But if you do, there is one obvious cooking tip: Always remember to remove the bell from the cat's collar before cooking." - Mike Royko

"Breathing in, I calm myself," Stuart recited to himself. "Breathing out, I am ready for whatever my destiny holds."

Many sessions of counseling had enabled Stuart to be able to pick up his life and live it after his mother's murder, which had totally altered his life's path. Now, however, he felt he was back in the throes of agony as in the days following his discovery of his mother Edna's body.

Susan's car jolted to a stop. Stuart yanked open the rear door, leapt to his feet and pushed his portly form toward the side of the building where Louise's apartment was located. He sped past several seniors carrying pans and casseroles. Intent on their mission, they, took rapid but mincing steps toward the community room to share their culinary talent and enjoy the company of their neighbors. Stuart could not have taken less notice of them, though he almost capsized a very elderly lady with a blue speckled roasting pan that seemed almost as big as she was.

The door to Louise's apartment was unlocked. That struck Stuart as a bit strange. Louise didn't have much in the way of worldly goods, but she was always protective of what she did own. The small apartment was disorderly, but not strangely so. The remnants of two salads sat on the kitchen table. Two? Louise had had company? Stuart wondered. Salads? Louise loved good food, but she was much of a culinary sort. She would never have splurged on the makings for fancy fruit salad. Something definitely was amiss.

"Louise! Louise!" he shouted. "Louise, are you here?" Again and again he repeated himself. Yes, she could already be at the pot luck. But knowing his sister's tendency to be late, he would have thought she'd still be fussing with her makeup.

Finally satisfied that Louise was definitely not in her apartment, Stuart hurried to the community room, deciding to take the stairs rather than wait for the elevator. He barely noticed that he was huffing and puffing heavily when he emerged from the stairwell into the community room and discovered two women beating furiously on the women's restroom door.

"Open up, in there."

"Are you all right?"

A third woman commented, "Sounds like she's being sick in there."

An elderly man in bib overalls hovered to the side of the hallway. Frail and hunched over, his dark eyes expressed great concern, and though his persona read severe *dementia*, he seemed to be trying to say something.

The wail of sirens pierced the air. Brakes screeched. Soon, heavy footsteps pounded the stairs. The heads of local firemen and local police emerged from the open doorway followed by EMS personnel. After barking a few questions, they turned to the bathroom door. When a quick knock received no response, a burly shoulder heaved the door from its moorings revealing the body of Louise lying next to the bathroom stool.

"Miss, can you hear me? Wake up, Miss," commanded the officer in charge. He kneeled down to check her pulse. Yes, there was still a faint pulse. An EMT sprang into action. Another EMT looked around to find someone who could answer.

Stuart peeked into the bathroom charged with chaos and excitement.

"Oh no! Oh no!" cried Stuart. He dropped to his knees beside Louise despite an attempt by the burly policeman to restrain him. "Louise, Louise, can you hear me? Please, squeeze my hand if you can hear me."

The EMT collecting data tapped Stuart on the shoulder to ask for Louise's medical information.

Stuart dully recited her full name, apartment number, height, weight, and the fact that she didn't have any known medical issues. He volunteered that Louise may have used a variety of recreation drugs in the past. To his knowledge she wasn't using anything other than alcohol at the present time.

"We need to get her to the hospital right now," the EMT kneeling beside Louise announced. "This is acting like heart failure. Could she have been poisoned? She sure as heck is trying to get rid of something."

"Let's move," said the EMT. "We've got to get her on a gurney."

"Will she make it?" Stuart asked timidly. "Can I ride in the ambulance with her?"

"And who are you?" asked a policeman.

"I'm her brother" Stuart answered defensively.

"Yeah, yeah, yeah," snapped the policeman. "How do I know you didn't poison her?"

"Me? Poison my own sister?" Stuart was shocked at the very idea. "You must be joking."

"This is no joking matter," replied the EMT. "This woman has been poisoned. She needs breathing support, her stomach pumped. Get some fluids into her, keep her heart going. Now move it, buddy."

Off to the side, Stuart heard the old man in the overalls mutter, "The oleander leaves. The oleander leaves. The man picked oleander leaves."

Stuart looked into the eyes of the elderly man and asked, "Are you sure?"

"Bad man", replied the vacant looking man, "I saw him. Picked leaves. Bad man. Bad man."

RHUBARB

"Why should we be in such desperate haste to succeed, and in such desperate enterprises? If a man does not keep pace with his companions, perhaps it is because he hears a different drummer." - Henry David Thoreau

Sirens really didn't bother Rhu anymore. The arrival of first, the firemen, then the policemen and the EMT squad hardly pierced his subconscious, let alone his conscious mind. This was typical distraction at senior properties. Someone was always tripping their pull cord by mistake, falling down and not being able to get up, or thinking they were having a heart attack. Rhu had learned long ago to ignore these sirens. Panic didn't enter his mind as he stood in Nancy's office.

Her composure crumbled. Was she that new to the job? Rhu really hadn't thought so. Hearing the clamor of footsteps, Nancy rose from her chair just as local firemen and EMT staff, already familiar with the building layout, raced up the stairway to the community room without wasting a step.

"My God, I wonder what's going on now?" exclaimed Nancy.

"Seems like business as usual at the old folk's home," Rhu chuckled.

"I don't think so," said Nancy. "Oh my! Here come Susan and Mary."

Rhu whipped his head around. Mary? And the Viking Bitch. He had already picked up Mary's term for Susan. Why on earth would they be here? This couldn't be good! Was Louise already sick? Had someone already called 911? That seemed unusually efficient, unless someone suspected foul play.

Panic quickly now entered his mind. He had to get out of there, and deftly slipped out the side door. Did Susan and Mary spot him? He wondered. He really didn't think so as he hurried to Big Bertha II. His fingers converged on a set of keys in his pocket. Louise's red Camaro. Yes. He still had her keys. Must get to it. Fast.

A side view of Mary's twitching animal print skirt headed toward the office, her legs pumping rapidly, sped Rhu's departure. Normally he would have paused and enjoyed the view. He appreciate looking at Mary even more than he enjoyed matching wits with her.

Slow down. Slow down. Rhu told himself. He realized instinctively that if he hurried, his motion would attract attention.

He slid into the driver's seat of the faded Camaro, inserted the key in the ignition, and turned it in one swift motion. No response. Darn it! Turned it again. Nothing. Gull darn it to hell! He slid his foot on the ignition and as gently as he could manage, rocked between turning the key and giving it some gas. This baby needed coddling. Shit. Come on, Baby. Let's go!

Ah-ah. He heard the mechanical catch release, music to his ears. Praise the Lord. Rhubarb Clarence Johnson was about to get away with murder again.

Nature photographer, David Tacke, pursues his passions for roaming and capturing the landscape from his home base in Lanesboro.

Rainbow trout leaping at the dam

The Root River falls at night

Geese at the falls

Brown trout leaping the falls at Lanesboro

The Nuterator
By Peggy Hanson & Frank Wright

The latest news around our house is that we are getting in touch with our inner squirrels. That does not mean that you will see me and Frank chasing each other around Sylvan Park or burying acorns. Sorry. It does mean that we are gathering and storing nuts for the winter. Black walnuts.

Black walnut trees are all around us, in town and in the woods. They are valued for their beautiful wood. And among the walnut cognoscenti they are equally valued for their nutritious and tasty nuts. Getting from the green or disintegrating blackening balls on the ground to nuts ready to grace our baked goods,

Frank Wright loading the Black Wal-Nuterator

candy or hot cereal is not for the timid or the lazy. We have found that the most dedicated fans of black walnuts usually are in their 70's or older. Most of them also have lived through times where taking a pass on free food was not an option.

The older folks also know that a person could do worse things with their time than pass an evening with a few friends or family around a table - cracking and picking nuts and maybe spinning a few yarns while they are at it. I am for a black walnut revival in SE Minnesota. There is no time to waste. In a few more years, many of the people who know what to do with a black walnut may have passed on, like our friend the late Marion Storhoff.

Frank Wright & Peggy Hanson of Lanesboro have been growing, gathering and cooking their way through the local flora & fauna for two decades.

Mildred Johnson Williamson's Crescent Cookies (Makes about 5 dozen)

This was my Grandma's recipe. If you don't have black walnuts you can substitute English walnuts or pecans.

1/2 pound butter

1 cup confectioners (powdered) sugar (plus extra for rolling baked cookies in)

1 t. vanilla

1/2 pound finely chopped black walnuts (lightly toasted first in a 325 degree oven for about 10 minutes)

2 1/4 cups flour

Cream butter and sugar. Add remaining ingredients. Shape into crescents. Bake 20-25 minutes in 350 degree oven. When cool roll in powdered sugar.

Marion was one of Frank's many black walnut mentors. 18 years ago she shared the nuts from her yard with Frank, along with her drying and cracking techniques. "I like to hit them right THERE with a hammer," she said, making sure Frank could see just the right spot.

Through trial and error, web searching and learning from mentors like Marion, Frank has gotten pretty efficient at hulling, washing, drying, cracking and picking the nuts. I work in the picking, freezing, cooking and baking department.

We made a big step forward when we found the machine that we call the NUTERATOR at an auction in Lime Springs, Iowa. It is a contraption clearly fabricated by a Norwegian bachelor farmer and it can hull a five gallon bucket of walnuts in 45 seconds. This beats driving over them with your pickup.

After hulling, the nuts are washed and spread out to dry for a couple of months before sealing up in 5 gallon buckets. They can be stored in the shell for many years and we like to age ours for one year before cracking. Black walnuts do need to be dried and stored somewhere where squirrels cannot find them. One of Frank's grandma mentors used to dry them under her bed in shallow sweater boxes.

We also have acquired a MASTER NUT CRACKER made by Gerald Gardner of Sarcoxie, Missouri. Hand operated, it can crack 600 nuts in an hour. Ours has become so popular we just bought a second one as a loaner. Marion would have loved it. Better than a hammer, especially if you have a lot of nuts. One five gallon pail = about 25 pounds or 1000 dried nuts = 5 quarts premium nutmeats= about 5 pounds of nuts. Figure on 2 person hours per pound to sort and pick out nutmeats.

Yes, you could buy this many nuts for about $90 at the Co-op – but then you would not have had *the complete squirrel experience.* And you would still have to come up with the cash.

So do not delay. Find a walnut mentor. Put on some old clothes and make like a squirrel. Winter is just around the corner.

Poems on Wings
By Roger C. Morris

Wingman

I lost my wingman
last night.

We were walking
down Payne Avenue
when he went into a dive.

Before I could call him back,
there was a MiG
on his tail.
She had no armour,
but was equipped with
weapons of mass distraction.

They disabled his
counter-measures,
and he spun out of control.

I knew he was a goner,
so I headed for home.

I'll look for his wreckage
in the morning…

Roger C. Morris, a retired computer technician and technical writer, lives in northeast Minneapolis where he grows tomatoes in a raised-bed garden and writes poetry, essays and fiction.

Iron Butterfly

I discovered
A new drink
Last night…
IRON BUTTERFLY!

Now I have an
Urge to pollinate
Just like the
Monarchs in my garden…

As I flit from
Blossom to blossom
The mountains in
Central Mexico
Are calling for me
To migrate…

Bar tender,
One more
Iron Butterfly
Please…

My Youthful Oncologist
By Pixie Youngdahl

Doodle by Pixie Youngdahl

Back in that surreal world of an oncology office, I am greeted by the perkiest adolescent practicing medicine. I suspect her mom drives her to work. She is clearly skilled and ever so competent but, really, how does a nurse with thirty years' experience take advice from someone with still flushed cheeks wearing a size eight skirt?

She makes with all the pleasantries then asks, "So, you are a nurse, you quit smoking for twenty-five years and started again. Why?" (Concerned smile.)

"Because I went to Paris for a week."

"Tsk. Well, I went to Paris for a week and I didn't start smoking."

"You weren't having enough fun. Try again!"

Goody for you, oh perfect one. You are too young to smoke anyway.

She reviewed all the meds she prescribed for side effects and I told her I had some pot I was going to try. Obviously, she has not dabbled there either. "I wish you hadn't told me that. I won't put it in your chart."

Pixie Youngdahl, a retired R.N. living a quiet life in rural southeast Minnesota, still has deep roots in her home town, Minneapolis. She is the author of *Arguments & Negotiations*, from LOST LAKE FOLK ART.

I'm not going to mention wine or she'll have me in a treatment program or put me under house arrest for being a senior delinquent. As she matures in her practice, she'll come to see that patients are whole people, not just those frightened things sitting in the chair. I hope I helped her with that lesson.

On a subsequent visit she asked, "How are those cigarettes?"

"Great."

She'll learn more effective ways to frame a question, too.

When my youthful oncologist is finished with the teenage, authority-resistant Pixie, she turns me over to the nurses for a poke and five hours of therapeutic poison. Surely the cauldrons are bubbling over with my magic potion. Port-a-cath was placed yesterday and it went well. The Versed-Fentynl IV cocktails are worth the price of the procedure.

My family and loved ones are making it clear they are not finished with me yet, so I guess I must buy the package. Fact is, I'm not done with them either. I'll pull up my big girl pants and do this thing.

The room is large and plush. Huge recliner with heated seat, TV with DVD. The staff is warm, welcoming and well trained in this specialty. Here we go. One poke into the port on my upper chest and some adjustments on the pump and the first of six rounds of poison starts coursing through my veins.

First is Prednisone and some Benadryl to ward off allergic reactions to the toxic medicine. Then the Taxol, which takes about three hours to run. This is followed by Carboplatin. At the end of the treatment, they actually drain each drop into me, though I know IV bags are always overfilled. I asked why. They reply, the stuff is too hazardous for the bio-medical waste so it's put in me instead. Doing my part to keep Minnesota green!

I am never alone, the book and the knitting I brought remain in my bag. My family hangs out and eats lunch. The staff are in and out frequently. The time does go by easily enough and I feel perfectly fine throughout. See, it's one of the tricks of the trade, fix it so they go home to be sick!

Arguments & & Negotiations

BEADRIN PIXIE YOUNGDAHL URISTA

Lost Lake Folk Art
Lanesboro

Destination Lanesboro
A careful look through Folk Opera Glasses

Lost Lake from Parkway Avenue

F irst met John Davis, Executive Director of the Lanesboro Art Center, on a memorably brittle winter night at a reading by half-a-dozen Minnesota poets held in the St. Mane Theater during Commonweal's 2000-2001 off-season. Probably pushing forty at the time, John's hair wasn't real long, as I recall, but faintly roguish and quite a bit darker than it is now, not so wintery. He had then, has still, the visage of a satisfied critter, eyes smiling from a woods on the Lost Lake shore, curious yet ambiguous, watching you carefully only until you look too long back into them. Combination of wile, etiquette and, I dare say, quiet reserve.

Like many folks, I reckon, who first met John while seeking a palliative at the *Cornucopia Art Center* – precursor to the LAC – I suffered a bad case of acute withdrawal from the well-endowed literary, museum, theater and concert scene out East, which I had left behind six months earlier to move to Bluff Country. A relative newcomer himself, having arrived in Lanesboro in 2000 towing a vintage Airstream trailer that had been home for the better part of two years, John asked me the sort of oblique questions a therapist might upon recognizing a distressed patient in need of discourse. Quickly learned we shared many interests, not least the arts, but also an appreciation of winter's beautiful brutality, confronting whenever possible on a pair of cross country skis. Out of the blue, John said, "We should ski sometime."

Never would reconnect to ski. But as years passed and the Grand Vision of Lanesboro came better into focus, I never forgot John's open invitation to venture somewhere new, on skis, on foot, in the imagination, an invitation no doubt to come visit the *campus* he'd been dreaming about.

Lanesboro Sales Commission stockyard

In a nutshell, to John Davis, Arts Campus vision is 'creative place-making'. He has already transformed one small, run-of-the-mill town facing the all too common woes of rural decline into a nationally recognized arts and culture center. If the word *campus* conjures up ivy on red brick, a quirky but quaint old-school teachers college, inspirational, cozy, then you've got the basic idea. Once acquisition and construction of

CORE VALUE:
"In order to thrive, the arts in America – and broad access to them – need an investment of a mix of public, private and consumer resources."
AMERICANS FOR THE ARTS

Phase 1 & 2 projects are completed, the $1.7 million Lanesboro campus will integrate an even more sustainable arts and theater culture with the expanding hospitality, retail, tourism, recreation sectors to produce a *destination*. In the economic calculus of creative place-making, the growth, the development of any community into a full-service destination is the ultimate economic solution. It is, to coin a phrase, the Holy Grail.

Many others were busy shaping Lanesboro into a destination back in 2000 when John took the helm at the *Cornucopia*. He came with a destination pedigree, having spent a decade on a similar creative place-making quest in New York Mills, MN. He quickly founded the Kids Philosophy Slam – a big idea that came to him between jobs – an Artist Residency program and Public Art. When the medallions commemorating local history created at the first Iron Pour in Sylvan Park cooled, John was just getting warmed up.

Stream of Thought Tour – 2006

Early community input and planning defined grant writing tasks and fundraising goals resulting in a $600,000 arts campus project Phase-1, now completed. There's a pedestrian walkway passes under County Highway 8 on the figurative left bank of the Root right where Townsite Company engineers in 1874 had trained the untamed river to flow north. Coffee Street Bridge, which the County 8 Bridge replaced, was renovated for pedestrian traffic as well. A local bank provided financing to purchase the historic Art Center gallery and office building. The City set aside public land for development of the Gateway Sculpture Park. Additional grants funded creation of park sculptures, the Artful Wayfinding System and acquisition of the St. Mane Theater after the Commonweal moved into its $3.2-million facility in the summer of 2007.

Through 2009, the Lanesboro Arts Council operated the St. Mane Theater; and therein, as the Bard so poetically pointed out, lies a tale. The Arts Council, established in 1981, eight years before the Root River State Trail opened, thirteen years before the *Cornucopia* and nearly twenty years before John was hired, had crafted its own arts and culture vision. With Arts Council help, Lanesboro reinvented itself, acquiring a nickname along the

Walking Bridge in fall

way that sounded much more inviting to prospective tourists than *Sewer City*, which, as legend goes, originated on the opposite olfactory end of Coffee Street from the walking bridge at the bustling, mooing and lowing Commission Sales livestock auction.

With Arts Council support, the Commonweal began producing plays in 1989, same year the trail opened. Art in the Park started under the Arts Council umbrella, and Over the Back Fence, a radio variety staple at the St. Mane for many years. With increasing tourism as its goal, in 1990 a tourism bureau opened at the St. Mane, providing a B&B booking service until the Chamber of Commerce, which is today extremely dynamic in its own right, took over every aspect of promoting Lanesboro's now diverse tourist market. Indeed, the tourist *menu du jour* seems to get longer every year as longtime residents and newcomers alike come up with *a la carte* items. Rhubarb Festival, the old west shoot 'em up during Buffalo Bill Days, Lanesboro Live radio and Ladies Day Out.

In 2008, the State legislature designated Lanesboro the Bed & Breakfast Capitol of Minnesota. Next, lawmakers dubbed it the Rhubarb Capitol of Minnesota. Since the early nineties, when it first made the honor roll of Top 100 Art Towns in America, Lanesboro routinely shows up on national "Best" lists and has frequently been the subject of national, state and local media features.

Today, well-endowed non-profits and prestigious foundations like the McKnight, Art Place, InnOvation, Minnesota Historical Society and the National Endowment for the Arts consider Lanesboro a paradigm for other communities in search of their own Lost Lake. "We find it's been a successful strategy," said John, modestly understating the obvious, "for the scope, the vision, the fundraising, the benefits of investing in the arts."

Investment, plenty of it too, has been critical. Lanesboro is a non-profit town. And if natural beauty and the wonder of arts are the magic in the *Magic Hamlet*, then 501(c)3 tax-exempt organizations – that arguably live or die according to the guidance of boards

Lanesboro has not had a grocery store since Village Foods closed in Dec-2008.

of directors and the altruism of donors private and public – are the nectar filling the Holy Grail. That said, the *Magic Hamlet* has had to weather an occasional disenchanting episode. Coordinating multiple events, raising funds, scheduling, ticketing, staffing, that's tricky enough. But realizing a complex vision, lots of moving parts, bringing old and new together, artists with farmers, newcomers with commuters who drive out of town for work every day passing tourists coming the other way on vacation: that can be daunting.

When a small town with fewer than 800 residents spawns two autonomous, non-profit arts organizations – three, counting the non-profit professional Commonweal Theater, which in terms of fundraising, ancillary programs and annual ticket sales that dwarfs the town's population, setting a five show attendance record of 22,440 in 2012, and is often and oddly compared to the Minneapolis Guthrie – management can be difficult at best, and at worst, inefficient, counterproductive and redundant. But don't say that too loudly or a twinkle might be misconstrued coming from your eye.

John arrived in Lanesboro towing not just a silver trailer but all the press, awards and well-deserved kudos he earned during a decade as the sparkplug of New York Mills. Among other things, NYM is where he started the renowned Great American Think-Off, established a Regional Arts Center in a dilapidated building, and is widely credited with creating seventeen new businesses and three hundred-fifty new jobs. WOW. Sure, there were volunteers and local leaders, but John had the vision to put a town of 1,000 souls, stranded somewhere northwest of Brainerd headed the long way to Fargo, on the map. USA Today branded NYM one of Culturally Coolest places to visit.

The non-profit market, Lanesboro Local filled the grocery vacuum in 2011

Shortly after he arrived here, John broached the delicate subject of merging *Cornucopia* with the Lanesboro Arts Council. Eventually, he pushed merger to the top of the coordination agenda and board members formally voted to reject his idea.

Born in New York City, schooled in Indiana, a Minneapolis College of Art and Design grad, in 1987 John bought an abandoned farm in Otter Tail County and supported himself painting houses. He's a fisherman, a free-spirit with a cozy trailer. So when merger failed to catch on, John left. In the fall of 2006, he took the Kids Philosophy Slam on the road, pulled the Stream of Thought south and west, spoke to other communities interested in his innovative ideas about arts, kids and rural renaissance.

When the arts, tourism, retail, hospitality and city government community – that would pretty much be the Whole Community, I guess – took another look at John's Grand Vision in the long shadow of the Great Recession, they asked him back. The two arts organizations agreed to merge and in 2010 the newly-formed LAC board hired John Davis to run it, lead it, break trail through deep snow going *thataway*: Phase-2, an additional $1.1 million toward the Arts Campus Destination vision coming this Spring.

"Where do you see the City in twenty-five years?" I asked the man more than one reporter has labeled a *bona fide* social entrepreneurship guru.

"That's for Lanesboro to decide," he replied, asking me a question. "What is ability of this arts community to contribute to the City?" John slowly withdrew to a cold thicket, his eyes, I'm guessing, fixed on something shiny perhaps in the deeps of Lost Lake.

12 Short Poems

From *i am alone facing the moon
rising on the edge of a mountain*
By Eddy J. Rathke

1.
blossoms floating
this lake reeks of dying beasts
birds soar & never –
don't let summer end this way
autumn will sing our lives away

2.
when it was too hot
we could not cool the house
now it's so very cold
there's no heat to comfort us
only blankets & sweaters

3.
clothes piled & dirty
i sleep in a basement-- dank
books fill space
& i dance over carpet
dreaming on my laptop

4.
redwine stained teeth
there were nights we drank too much
mornings we slept too much
dying for your touch   cold couch
old skin dusts awaybut you –

**Eddy J. Rathke edits for *The Lit Pub*,
interviews for *Monkey Bicycle*, and
reviews for a variety of publications.
The author in 2012 of *Ash Cinema*,
KUBOA, he lives in the Twin Cities.**

5.
my teeth grind
on the bones of the earth
lift my muddy face
show me the sun again
don't leave me drowning on dirt

6.
sometimes I pretend –
planting trees in autumn
– don't let it wither
reading books in trees alone
mobilize the radical

7.
an uprooted tree
the storm rends the earth but--
it leaves us dry
today washed clean & renewed
earth's pain & horror dissolves

8.
drinking for mourning
spirits burn my throat
moths emerge with sinister eyes
my room is their cocoon

9.
the still night –
the low hum of insects
the barking dog

10.
when birds sing
we try to capture their beauty
not content to just hear

11.
in the journey to the sky
there was a hole
i fell through

12.
tongues like flitting wings
but let's change history
together   today

Winterlake
By Lisa Lundquist

The casket had pink satin lining, the only one with any color at all, so I chose it. My mom had told me years before, "I hate wearing white, it makes me look dead. Promise me, no white lining in my casket!" We laughed. Who wants to look dead in her coffin?

Illness came out of nowhere. Mom'd been fine that morning. We chatted on the phone about her job, about who was feuding with whom in her church circle, about the neighbors of course. That evening, a friend of mom's, Marie, called me. "Kathy, your mother is in the hospital, it's a brain tumor." I couldn't process what Marie was saying. "What? What are you talking about? I spoke to her this morning. She was fine."

Lisa Lundquist has been a reader since she could first hold a book, and writer since she was twelve. She lives in Rochester, MN.

Marie explained she'd been visiting when suddenly Mom started to shake uncontrollably, her speech became slurred. "I thought she was having a stroke!"

Mom's surgeon recommended treatment, but he made it clear that with or without chemo, sometime in the next six months, I would be an orphan.

My dad died when I was ten. A motorcycle accident. It'd been just Mom and me ever since.

Mom faced her death the way she did her life, with humor. We had lots of laughs those last few months. And some tears, too. I found the thought of life without my mom excruciating. And when she said, "I knew I should have weaned you," I laughed and cried simultaneously.

"The funeral's pre-paid," she said. "I told Scotty at Andersen Funeral Home that I'd lie in the front hall when it was time, make it easier to haul me out." Mom, always thinking of others.

She slept a lot toward the end. One gray afternoon, Mom woke from her nap and abruptly announced, "Kathy, I killed a baby."

"Mom, you had a bad dream. Go back to sleep."

"No," she insisted, her voice unsteady but clear. "I killed a baby."

I froze. "No, Mom, come on. What do you mean? You didn't kill a baby. I mean, God. You're dreaming."

"David Donaldson and I – we'd taken the bus to the State Fair for the fireworks. In 1966, I was thirteen, Dave was eighteen. We weren't dating or anything. My parents wouldn't have allowed it. They thought I was out with the girls, you know, Bev Dahl and Marge Erickson. I knew Dave from

school. We rode the bus home together, got Cokes sometimes, until he graduated and joined the Army. Very innocent. Dave was always a gentleman. But that night … he was … so determined. He was going to Viet Nam in a few weeks. Maybe that was part of it." She broke off. "But I didn't try to stop him. Oh, God, I wanted him to kiss me. I could have said no. I didn't. It wasn't anything. I was so surprised. I thought, Is this what all the fuss is about? It was so … so nothing. Sex was embarrassing, if anything." Mom's eyes were glued to mine. "Dave didn't come home from the war."

"You got *pregnant*?" I screeched, my voice suffused with shock.

"I had no earthly clue how a girl got pregnant!" Mom shrieked, "None. There was no sex education back then. It took me months to understand what was happening inside my own body. I couldn't go to a doctor. He would have told my mother," she sobbed.

I grabbed her hand, held it tight.

"When I finally faced the fact that I was going to have a baby at thirteen, I never once considered that I was going to be a mother. In my mind, I was *not* going to be a mother. I was going to have a baby, yes, and I was far too young for that."

"Mom, what did you *do*?" This lady, my own mother, church-goer, the person who always thought of others first, this *saint*, her story astounded me.

"I answered an ad in *Good Housekeeping*, two brothers – bachelors – looking for a live-in housekeeper near Anchorage, Alaska. Bud and Dennis Branham. I sent them a letter and lied, told them I was twenty, that I'd kept house for my widowed father. I said I wanted the adventure of traveling to

Alaska." She let go a strangled laugh mixed with another painful sob. "Adventure! All I wanted was to be a nice, normal girl. I didn't want any more adventure! I wanted to marry a nice boy! Not that a nice boy would have me, not after getting pregnant at thirteen."

Mom wiped her eyes. "I snuck out of my parents' house in the middle of the night. Left a note behind saying I was going to Mackinac Island, that I'd gotten a job as a maid. I knew my mother would be so angry. She wouldn't let my dad try to find me. I knew I was burning my bridges.

"Turned out, the brothers didn't actually live in Anchorage. They lived in the middle of nowhere. It was so remote. We had to take a float plane. Incredible scenery, but I was so afraid. I'd never been on a plane; it was so rickety. I kept thinking – hoping – we'd crash into the mountains. I wouldn't have to own up about the baby or admit to the brothers that I didn't know the first thing about being a housekeeper."

"Mom … don't."

She ignored me. "They were sweet, the brothers. Dennis had this grimy red bandanna he always wore around his neck. He said it made him look French. We'd laugh at him. And Bud had a bushy brown beard, and the biggest belly laugh. They were good people. The house – a shack really – perched on the edge of Winterlake facing the Tordrillo Mountains. There were two islands in the lake, and you could row out and pick wonderful blueberries. That's where I learned to make my blueberry muffins.

"I wasn't really showing the first few weeks, I was chubby, but I covered up with big sweaters. Wasn't too long though before Bud and Dennis knew. They were happy! They were so naïve, they thought we all could live together there on Winterlake. Dennis used to say he'd take 'the little nipper' fishing, that he'd teach him to hunt. Then he'd add, 'It's okay if it's a girl, Shirley. Nothin' wrong with a girl.' Bud would laugh and say 'Damn right, nothin' wrong with a girl! She'll be the prettiest gal in the whole state!' They were so excited, like they'd planned the whole thing, bringing me up there and all.

"The bigger I got, the more frantic I got. There was no doctor nearby. The thought of dying in childbirth terrified me. Plus, you won't believe this, I mean, I'd already proven I was a slut, but, I didn't want the brothers to see me, you know, that way. Exposed." Mom's laugh held no mirth.

"Turned out I didn't need to worry. A wildfire broke out a few miles from the cabin. If the wind shifted, we'd be in its path. So we packed everything valuable into the rowboat, just in case.

Wasn't much. The brothers – everyone called them that; I always thought it made them sound like monks – had a few pieces of sterling from their mother. I certainly didn't have anything. But, anyway, Bud and Dennis were away fighting the fire when the baby came.

"I squatted for the longest time in the kitchen after a quick birth, the slimy little thing lying on the floor. It didn't really look like a baby. More like a … creature. Eventually, I cut the cord with Bud's hunting knife. Didn't want to touch the creature. It was so … gunky." Mom gulped air. "There was so much blood."

I didn't know how to respond. This was my *mother* talking, the most responsible woman in the world!

She continued. "The creature cried, once. I didn't want to listen. I didn't want it to be a person. Kathy, can you understand that? I did *not* want that baby to be a person. I wanted it gone. Just gone." Tears streamed down her face.

"You didn't kill the baby." I heard myself pleading, practically breathless. "Mom, you didn't kill the baby."

"It was a boy, Bud told me. I hadn't looked at it that closely. When they came home, it was still on the floor, still so bloody. I guess, I mean, I know it had stopped breathing by then. Dennis picked it up so tenderly, his voice gentle when he told me it was dead. The thought never occurred to either of them that I had killed it despite all that blood. Bud and Dennis were naive too. They didn't know what childbirth was like. They believed it had been stillborn. Bud cried."

I tried to stop her there. "Mom, please."

"They said we had to bury it. I told then to do whatever they wanted. I didn't care. That finally shocked them. But I guess they thought I was upset. Really, I was just so glad to be rid of it. Free. My life could begin again.

"We never talked about it. I know the brothers thought they were being kind. I didn't care. About a month later, I went over to the little island to get blueberries for a pie. I saw the cross stuck in the ground. They'd carved Baby Harry, July 27, 1964 on it. The brothers' father was named Harry. Dennis had tied his red bandanna around the cross. Until I saw the grave, I hadn't once worried about what they did with it. Baby Harry." Mom took a deep breath and exhaled long and tired. "I'm going to hell, Kathy."

I knew, later, I would think more clearly about what my mother claimed happened at Winterlake. But right at that moment, I felt she needed the support she hadn't had at thirteen.

"Mom, you didn't kill Baby Harry!" I leaned over the bed, tears welling in my eyes, and hugged her. "It, just, Baby Harry, Mom, he just died."

Mom gently pushed me back, nodded. "I've told myself that for over forty years, Kathy. It just died. True enough. But I was stabbing at it with a hunting knife when it did."

The Tortoise and the Hare

By Nancy Overcott

Coneflower - drawing by Dana Gardner

One can learn a lot about a marriage by watching how a couple works together. Art and I just finished gathering our winter supply of firewood. At the beginning, we were nervous about our cranky backs because every part of the process, from cutting trees to stacking the wood, involves backbreaking labor. Once started, though, we ignored the pain, the sweat dripping into our eyes, even the bee stings.

We planned to cut medium sized trees around the periphery of a field adjacent to our house to make more room for grassland birds and wildflowers, like the yellow coneflowers that had just finished blooming there. We knew better than to cut big heavy trees deep in the woods as we had done in our younger years.

Deciding which trees to cut was harder than expected. When we saw sapsucker holes in neat little rows, we felt sad about depriving the sapsucker of its nectar. When we saw dead branches reaching into the sky, we felt sad about depriving hawks of their perches. Some trees were old friends. At one time, we didn't worry about these things, but over the years, we have become increasingly sensitive to the needs of other woodlanders.

Nancy Overcott, Preston, MN, is the author of many books and essays including *Fifty Common Birds of the Midwest* and *Fifty Uncommon Birds of the Midwest*, University of Iowa Press, and most recently, *Living in a Dream* from LOST LAKE FOLK ART.

In felling a tree, the first step was to cut a pie-shaped chunk from one side to insure that it would fall in the right direction. The next step was to cut on the opposite side until the tree came down. I watched as Art cut the first tree. Clearly, his skill had improved over the years. The chainsaw wasn't stuck and the tree fell as planned.

Next, he cut the smaller branches while I hauled them away. This was the part where Art used to criticize me for not hauling the branches fast enough or in the right direction. It felt like he not only didn't appreciate all the work I was doing, but that he also expected me to read his mind.

We have both changed over the years. This year I found that I could almost read my husband's mind if I paid close attention. I decided to let him be the boss since he has more skill in this area than I do. For his part, although he sometimes seemed exasperated with me, a new patience was also apparent.

The next step was to make stove length cuts in the trunk and larger branches. When Art finished the upper cuts, I rolled the logs over and held them in place so he could finish the job. Then, I busied myself throwing the wood into the wagon until he required my assistance again.

When the wagon was full, Art pulled it to the log splitter by the woodshed. We lifted the larger sizes of wood together and placed them on the splitter. As the pieces came off the splitter, we threw them on a pile along with the smaller pieces.

We didn't need words for these maneuvers. Our ability to coordinate our tasks while anticipating each other's needs felt good.

When it came time to stack the wood, we tried to do it together, but our work styles finally collided. I like to work slowly, methodically placing each log in just the right place, and not resting until I complete the job. Art's style is to work fast, rest, and then work fast again. I am the tortoise; he is the hare. He soon left the stacking to me and went to push the leftover brush to the periphery of our yard.

Although we can sometimes work as one, it is apparent that we are still individuals with our own styles. Over the years, without realizing when it began to happen, we have learned to compromise when it matters and when it doesn't, we work and play according to our separate personalities.

We worked for five days. At the end of each workday, we sat silently on the porch listening to the birdsong that replaced the sounds of the chainsaw, tractor and log splitter.

Our yard looks different now. The cutting of trees has changed the play of light and shadow. The birds, squirrels and chipmunks forage in the new piles of brush. When we look out our kitchen window at our well-stocked woodshed, we see more than a supply of fuel for the winter; we see a history of our life together.

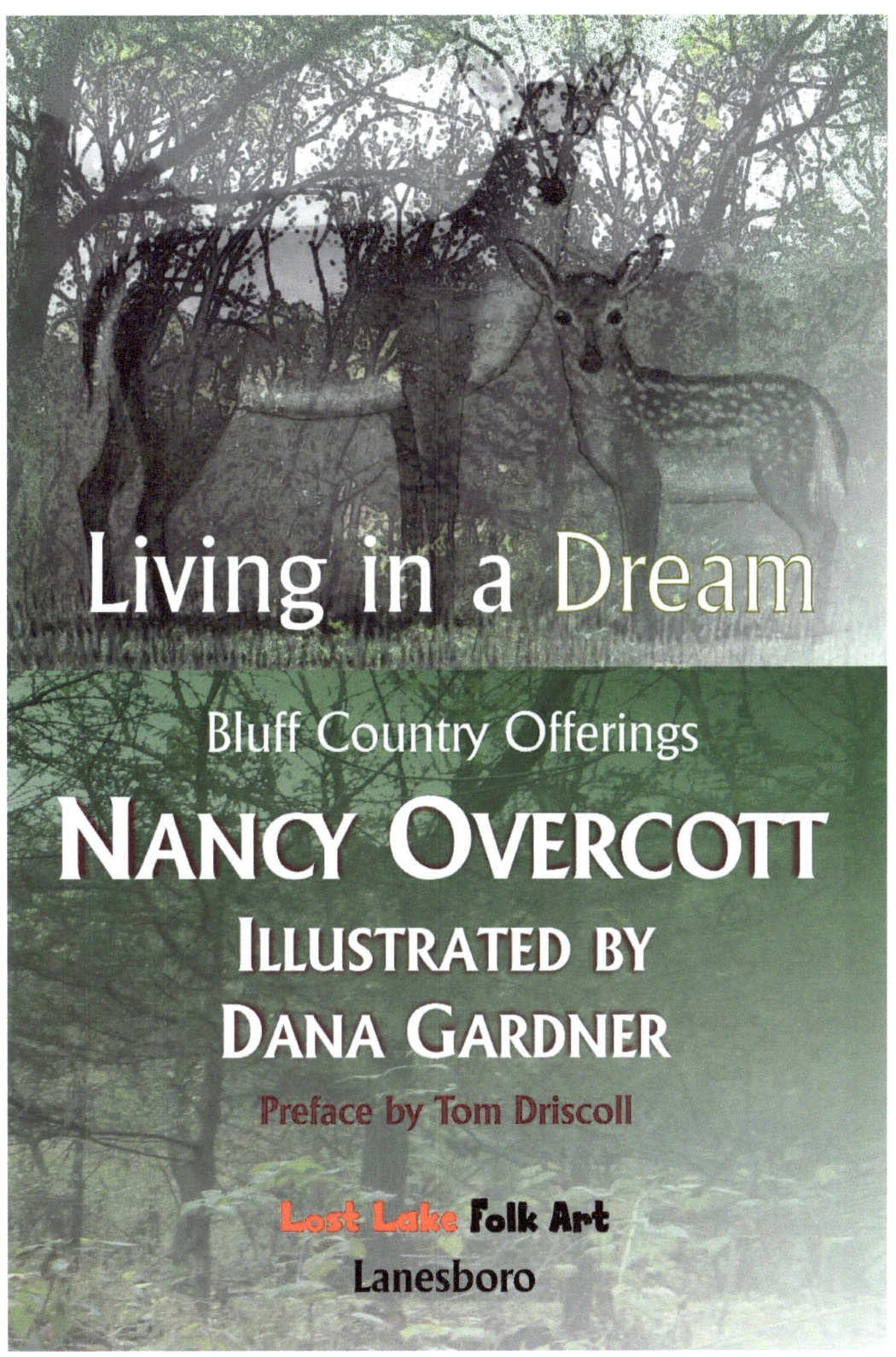

Living in a Dream

Bluff Country Offerings

NANCY OVERCOTT

ILLUSTRATED BY
DANA GARDNER

Preface by Tom Driscoll

Lost Lake Folk Art

Lanesboro

Four of Things
Poems by Anne Barngrover

Thing of Beauty

Chicken skin bunched to the knob

Of a drumstick. Prepackaged

strawberry flower. Light gunned

down in green rows: cathedral

Of pecan. Anyone says *let go now*,

but look at how the world

holds on: in the dollarweed, last

hound bayed to night's deep.

From a bucket, last crawfish

twitched before boil.

Without you near, I am the hard-

faced shed with a heart

of blue rot. I am home to rat snake

Anne Barngrover's poems have appeared in *Indiana Review, Meridian, Smartish Pace* and others. She holds an MFA from Florida State University and is currently a PhD candidate in English at University of Missouri. A new collection, *Yell Hound Blues*, will be available in December from UP ON BIG ROCK POETRY SERIES.

      & shutter-vine. Take

your apologies to your religion.

      See what miracles you can

perform this time. Things

      that fester are built to last

it all: through a controlled

      burn, through a civil war.

Thing of Blame

These brown sand dollars piss
    along the truck bed. Boiled
peanuts blister in their Styrofoam.
    I'm burned in finger marks,
blued where fingers cannot go.
    Someone locked that dog
in a chicken coop. Someone
    swiped the zipper peas & swan
eggs, too. Spring-heeled Jack,
    they call him. His hooves track
over roofs of barns. He follows sin
    on his hind legs to a crossroads.
You'd better pray to an appleheaded
    dog. Your ass had better be ditch-
grown. A thing cast out was once
    too much desired. Drive me
away if you feel it so. I'm still
    the red of your dirt road.

Thing of Bone

Bloodspot knuckles into pale pink
    lace. Lips split in their corners.
How can I bargain with you when
    I want you still? Out-cry
the loud barred owls. Thumbprint
    the soft part of my thigh. I have
been to a church that was made of bones.
    Fingers spelled scripture. Skulls
lay rough-bunched behind bars.
    Things of ancient madness:
a blind monk scavenged gravesites.
    You begged scab-eyed,
naked on wet floor. Enough begets
    enough. I will baptize my daughter
in sink water on the day she is born.
    I will blow my breath into the tiniest
bones of her innermost ear,
    bones hidden even from God.

Thing of Blues

Tree frogs swell the rainfall

    with snapping rubber bands.

Mimosas doze, blushing

    poms. Millipedes pretend

they're trains transecting ferns'

damp slough. Such are the days

I miss the deep sadness

    I have known: dead breaths

stamped in gravel, haunting us.

    The woods will serve as my

confessional when I say I am

    not guiltless. Hardest to forgive,

this: that I reaped a thousand seasons

    for his heart. Where was it

in the pile, deer-picked & overripe?

    Fogs lift from steel tracks

after rainstorm. New love, you must

    believe: I'm letting go

another thousand times,

    a thousand ways or more.

Opinion: Everybody has one
By Tom Driscoll

In my *opinion*, it's not the fact that you have an opinion that matters. What matters is what you make of your opinion. **Folk Opera** magazine is not interested in publicizing artifice, clever wordplay used to cloak shallow views, derivative judgments or NSA fodder. When it comes to opinion, **Folk Opera** is interested in the Art of opinion, capital A, and we enthusiastically invite yours. Sound off, make a difference.

Opinion as an art form – a thing of elegant simplicity, simple complexity, a problematic argument articulated beautifully, beautiful rage rendered reasonable, etcetera, etcetera – definitely trumps unrefined opinion, raw emotion, unbridled passion, the knee jerk, the gut check, the scorching rhetorical devices deployed to distract from an idea's clear revelation.

Folk Opera will consider letters to the editor, opinion pieces and unsolicited feature articles of up to 3,000 words, and invites you to tackle just about any issue relevant to thoughtful readers so long as you don't proselytize, spew invective, repeat Internet twaddle, media sound bites, political platitudes or otherwise fail to think clearly and crisply when you make your case. Write down what you have to say, then read what you've written, then rewrite it as necessary before you hit send. After all, if you can't change the world, at least you can bake us a tasty pie.

SHIPWRECKT BOOKS PUBLISHING COMPANY

Raising independent publishing to the same level as Indie Music and Film

Our imprints:

Rocket Science Press
    * for authors of quality literary fiction

Up On Big Rock Poetry Series
    * giving voice to new and powerful bards

Lost Lake Folk Art
    * Everybody has a story to tell. Let us help you tell yours.

& is about out of silence an emergent cacophony of image, of imagination & is about the poets who carry sounds one at a time like precious sparks to the hearth: words cupped in their blistering hands, their impatient breaths keeping alive light & heat & racket.

> & the sky turns dark greenish
> if it were a bottle filled
>
> with purpled wine & instead of
> horizon there is this space
>
> crammed if it is your mind
> with your thoughts if they are
> the stars

Lanesboro